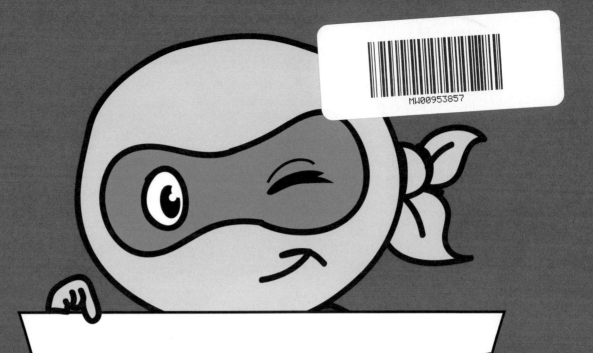

This book belongs to

_____

This book is dedicated to my children – Mikey, Kobe, and Jojo.
I'm sorry for what I said when I was hangry.

Hangry Ninja

A Book About Preventing Hanger and Managing Meltdowns and Outbursts

Ninja Life Hacks
by Mary Nhin

Hi, I'm Hangry Ninja. I'm very grateful to my friend, Angry Ninja, who taught me a useful strategy to control my anger.

The problem was that I experienced anger more often than I liked.

For example, when I hadn't had breakfast, I snapped at my family members for the smallest things.

After school, my fuse was shorter than normal, and I exploded if things didn't go a certain way.

Right before dinner, I argued with my siblings and ended up having a meltdown.

I got angry a lot.

Now, I want to share with you another emotion we experience – HANGER.

We experience hanger when we are hungry and angry at the same time. When we don't eat at regular intervals, our blood sugar gets low.

We can prevent hanger from happening if we remember the 4+3 rule.

This means you eat the four food groups, every three hours.

Some good examples of snacks or meals include:

- vegetable and turkey soup
- hummus and carrots with pinenuts and pita bread
- rice, chicken, and broccoli
- steak, potatoes, and carrots
- peanut butter, beet, and strawberry smoothie

Modified Version (when veggies are not available)

3 + 3 Rule

Eat 3 food groups every 3 hours.
Proteins
Carbs
Fats

The next day, I was doing somersaults in the living room with my brother. When he accidentally hit me with his feet while doing a flip, I felt my muscles tighten, my eyes swell up, and my breathing get heavier.

Do you know what happened next?

I told myself to breathe.
Then, I took three deep breaths and counted to ten.

While counting, I remembered that I last ate at 11 a.m.
I glanced at the clock.

*I ate three hours ago. The 4 + 3 strategy says we should
eat 4 food groups every 3 hours. So let me try it,* I thought.

Do you think the strategy worked?

Yes, it did!

My brother and I resolved our conflict over a bacon, avocado, tomato sandwich that we split in half.

Remembering the 4+3 rule could be your secret weapon against hanger.

Check out the Hangry Ninja lesson plans that contain fun activities to support the social, emotional lesson in this story at ninjalifehacks.tv!

I love to hear from my readers.
Write to me at info@ninjalifehacks.tv or send me mail at:

Mary Nhin
6608 N Western Avenue #1166
Oklahoma City, OK 73116

 @officialninjalifehacks

 @marynhin @officialninjalifehacks
#NinjaLifeHacks

 Mary Nhin   Ninja Life Hacks

 Ninja Life Hacks

Made in United States
Troutdale, OR
11/23/2024

25217062R00019